FDNY 2001-2011:
A Decade of Remembrance and Resilience

They are all gone into the world of light,
And I alone sit lingering here;
Their very memory is fair and bright,
And my sad thoughts doth clear.
— Henry Vaughan

This book is dedicated to the 343 members of the FDNY lost at the World Trade Center on September 11, 2001; and to the men and women of the Department who took part in our recovery and rebuilding.

M.T. Publishing Company, Inc.
P.O. Box 6802
Evansville, Indiana 47719-6802
www.mtpublishing.com

All Fire Department City of New York logos and marks depicted herein are property of the City of New York and may not be reproduced without consent.
Copyright © 2011
City of New York
All rights reserved.

Library of Congress Control Number:
2011928332

ISBN: 978-1-934729-62-5

Edited by:
Steve Ritea and Jenny Holland

Graphic Design by:
Thomas Ittycheria

Pre-press and publishing:
M.T. Publishing Company, Inc.
Evansville, IN

No part of this publication may be translated, reproduced, or transmitted in any form or by any means, electronic or mechanical, including photocopying and recording, or by any information storage and retrieval system, without expressed written permission of the copyright owner and M.T. Publishing Company, Inc.

The materials for this book were compiled and produced using available information. Although every reasonable effort has been made to be as accurate as possible about descriptions of events and photos, discrepancies in recorded history and human error are always possible; therefore, neither M.T. Publishing Company, Inc. nor anyone involved with the creation of this book shall be held responsible for any inaccuracies in the content.

Printed in the
United States of America

Table of Contents

Dedication 3

Introduction by President George W. Bush.................6

Father Mychal Judge 8

September 11, 2001 10

The World Trade Center Ribbon Campaign 36

The Last Beam Recovery 66

Faces of the Fallen 74

Commissioner's Message...78

Line of Duty Deaths Since September 11, 2001........80

Rebuilding the Ranks 81

Crash of American Airlines Flight 587.......................82

Staten Island Ferry Crash 84

Fighting Fires 86

Drills: Preparing for the Worst...................................90

East Side Crane Collapse...92

FDNY on the Water...94

Giving Back: FDNY Responds to Hurricane Katrina..96

Helping Haiti 99

Miracle on the Hudson 102

September 11th Families Making a Difference 104

Carrying on a Proud Legacy 106

Moments of Remembrance....................................107

Acknowledgements 112

FDNY 2001-2011: *A Decade of Remembrance and Resilienc*

Introduction by President George W. Bush

The attacks of September 11, 2001, changed our Nation forever. It was a day of unspeakable tragedy that America will never forget, and it was also a day of hope and heroism defined by citizens and rescuers who gave their lives to save others.

In our darkest hour, their sacrifice inspired the world and revealed the true character of America: generous, brave, and always prepared to serve the cause of righteousness.

For me, that morning began in Florida. I was sitting in a classroom listening to children read. Before entering the classroom, I had learned that a plane had crashed into the World Trade Center. We had very little information at first – even on the size of the plane – and I assumed it was a tragic accident.

As the children were reading, my Chief of Staff, Andy Card, whispered in my ear, "A second plane has hit the second tower. America is under attack."

My immediate reaction was outrage. *How dare someone attack our country?* Then I looked at the innocent children – and the media in the back of the room – and knew I had to project calm. If I panicked, it would send a signal of panic to the rest of the world.

At the appropriate time, I left the classroom and made a brief statement to the Nation about the attacks. Moments later, I was in the Presidential limousine heading toward Air Force One. My national security advisor, Condoleezza Rice, called and told me a third plane had crashed into the Pentagon. At that moment, there was no question in my mind: America was at war.

The brave men and women of the Fire Department of New York were among the first ground troops of that war. Hundreds of firefighters charged into the twin towers, not knowing if they would ever come out. Many did not.

They hauled heavy equipment and faced severe communications difficulties. But that did not stop them from making the long climb up to the impact zone. Their goal: to rescue as many of their fellow citizens as possible.

Scripture tells us that "Greater love has no one than this, that someone lay down his life for his friends." The first responders were true to that calling. The heroism and selflessness of the FDNY shined for the entire world to see.

I had a chance to see the spirit of the FDNY up close when I visited Ground Zero on September 14. The wreckage was still smoldering. The emotions were raw. I felt like I was walking through hell.

One soot-covered firefighter looked me square in the eye and said, "George, find the bastards who did this and kill them." It's not often that people call the president by his first name. But that was fine by me. This was personal.

I wanted to a send a message of support to the rescue workers and hopefully rally their spirits. I stepped atop a mound of metal and put my arm around firefighter Bob Beckwith.

Using a bullhorn, I started to address the crowd. People shouted, "We can't hear you!" I shouted back, "I can hear you! The rest of the world hears you. And the people who knocked these buildings down will hear all of us soon!" The crowd exploded. It was a release of energy I had never felt before.

I had many occasions to visit with members of the FDNY throughout my Presidency. I was always impressed with the decency, professionalism, and dedication of those I met.

Our Nation must never forget the 343 members of the Fire Department lost on September 11, 2011. For the families, friends, and colleagues of these heroes, their loss is a wound that will never heal. But they can always be proud knowing their loved ones died saving others – and in doing so, showed the world that America's spirit can never be shattered.

I appreciate the FDNY Foundation for assisting the department in its mission. On this solemn anniversary, I ask for God's blessings on the members of the FDNY and their families. May God continue to bless the United States of America.

"This is a blessed place, because God's work is being done from this house and in this house. And without you he can't do what he has to do save lives in this area…We're in a new century…100 years from now, who knows what this will all be about? None of us, we can't begin to visualize or realize. But God knows…It will all come back and then pass again. That's the way it is: Good days, bad days. Up days, down days. Sad days, happy days. But never a boring day on this job. You do what God has called you to do: You show up, you put one foot in front of another, you get on the rig and you go out. You do the job, which is a mystery and a surprise. You have no idea when you get on that rig – no matter how big the call, no matter how small – you have no idea what God's calling you to, but he needs you. He needs me. He needs all of us…"

— *FDNY Chaplain Father Mychal Judge*
at the dedication of Engine 73/Ladder 42
in the Bronx on Sept. 10, 2001

FDNY 2001-2011: *A Decade of Remembrance and Resilience*

"We get on the rig. We're going down. The probie, John Tierney, he was off duty before we got out. Something wasn't right that day. I knew something was wrong and I turned to him and said, 'John, do me a favor, don't take this run in. Just stay here. You're off duty, you're not getting paid. Just go home, man. Just go home.' But who is not going to jump on the rig? So he jumped on the rig."

— *Firefighter Bertram Springstead*

* Probationary Firefighter John Tierney was among the 343 FDNY members killed on Sept. 11, 2001

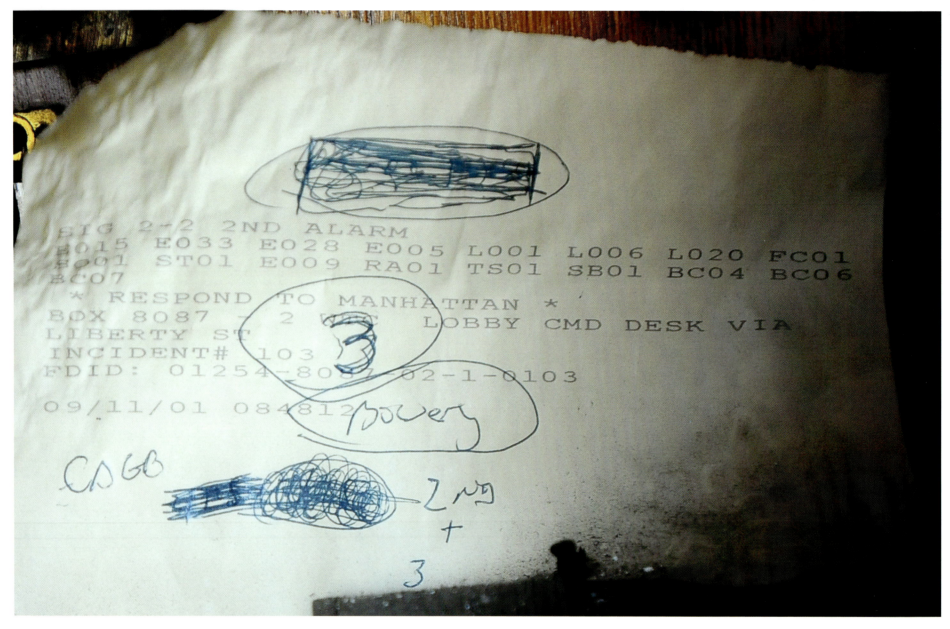

"Sometime about 8:15 or so in the morning we got a call to Lispenard and Church for a gas leak in the street. We were there for a while checking on the gas leak and then we heard the loud roar of the plane come over and we turned around and we looked and we saw the plane coming down, heading south toward the Trade Center and [it] made a direct hit on the Trade Center…I saw it hit. Within about ten seconds after that or so I gave the first report on the radio and transmitted a second alarm for a plane into the Trade Center."

— *Chief Joseph Pfeifer*

FDNY 2001-2011: *A Decade of Remembrance and Resilience*

"I could hear myself…go, 'Oh my God, no, no, no, no' and they were jumping...I've seen people jump as high as 25 stories, but that was very different…Here, with four times the height, it was kind of an, 'Oh my God, oh my God, oh my God.'"

— *Dr. Glenn Asaeda,
Division Medical Director*

Chief Gerard Barbara directing operations in front of the Marriott Hotel, at approximately 9:30 am. Chief Barbara was killed in the collapse of the South Tower at 9:59 am.

"We saw the jumpers coming. We didn't know what it was at first, but then the first body hit and then after that we knew what it was…I felt like I was intruding on a sacrament. They were choosing to die and I was watching them and shouldn't have been, so me and another guy turned away…."
— *Retired Firefighter Maureen McArdle-Schulman*

"We made our way up somewhere between the 15th and 20th floor, at which time we saw one woman…with burns along her arms. In the same vicinity we were met with a woman who was having severe respiratory distress…She was with a civilian who stated he was from the 90th floor…I questioned the guy from the 90th floor, who said it was a plane. That's when I first realized that we had a plane up there. He said there was a fireball on the 90th floor…"
— *Captain Gregg Hansson*

"I made it up as high as the 22nd floor and about that time…I think my men were maybe on the 20th floor and I started to come down and, at that point in time, I just said, 'It's time to go.' The stairway still had civilians in it and they were still moving out and we took whatever civilians we could take with us downstairs. We were not leaving them behind. I mean, we were not passing them to get out of the building. It was painfully slow going down and, in my mind – again, this is only my perception, my intuition – I just kept telling myself, 'I'm running out of time to get out of the building.'"
— Lieutenant Thomas Piambino

"I saw Father Judge...on West Street. And I saw him come out and I walked up to him, gave him a smile. I told him, 'Father Judge, we are going to need a lot of help here. You better get some more chaplains.' He smiled and said something. I don't remember what he said. That was the last time I saw him."
– Fire Commissioner Salvatore J. Cassano

The body of FDNY Chaplain Father Mychal Judge being carried away from the World Trade Center

"We were on the 30th or 31st, 32nd floor or something like that...when there was a very loud roaring sound and a very loud explosion...It really felt like our building was coming down and then the chief, who was out of sight for a few minutes, then came running up the stairs and that's my impression, and he was saying, 'All right' - everybody was very adamant and loud, and he said, 'Everybody, we are - all Fire Department personnel are out of the building. We are getting out. Leave all your equipment.' He was yelling, 'Leave your equipment and just get up and go, go, go'..."
— *Retired Captain Brian Becker*

The following is a transcript of the radio communications between members of Battalion 7, Battalion 9 and Ladder 15, which provides the only known account of what was happening on the upper floors of Tower 2 immediately prior to its collapse. Led by Battalion 7 Chief Orio Palmer, (left), a twenty-year veteran of the FDNY, the men captured in this recording displayed remarkable calm and bravery amidst horror. The tapes show they remained focused on rescuing civilians even though conditions were dire. Chief Palmer reached the impact zone at the 78th floor. All the members on this recording were killed in the collapse.

The following members were communicating with Chief Palmer throughout the transmission. All were killed in the collapse:

**Battalion 9 Chief
Edward Geraghty**

**Ladder 15 Lieutenant
Joseph Leavey**

**Firefighter
Scott Kopytko**
Ladder 15 *(Roof)*

**Firefighter
Thomas Kelly**
Ladder 15 *(OV)*

**Firefighter
Scott Larsen**
Ladder 15 *(Irons)*

**Firefighter
Doug Oelschlager**
Ladder 15 *(Can)*

**Battalion 7 Aide
Firefighter
Stephen Belson**

**Battalion 9 Aide
Firefighter
Alan Feinberg**

**Fire Marshal
Ronald Bucca**

9:24 a.m.
Ladder 15: "Go ahead, Irons."
Ladder 15 Irons: "Just got a report from the director of Morgan Stanley. [Floor] 78 seems to have taken the brunt of this stuff, there's a lot of bodies. They say the stairway is clear all the way up, though."
(Irons refers to a member of Ladder 15 who carries the axe and other tools)
Ladder 15: "Alright, 10-4 Scott. What, what floor are you on?"
Ladder 15 Irons: "48 right now."
Ladder 15: "Alright, we're coming up behind you."

9:31 a.m.
Battalion 7 Aide *(7 Alpha)*: "Battalion 7, you want me to relay?"
Ladder 15: "Yeah, Steve, tell Chief Palmer they got reports that there's more planes in the area. We may have to back down here."
Battalion 7 Aide: "10-4. 7 Alpha to 7."
Battalion 7 Chief: "Steve. 7 to 7 Alpha."
Ladder 15: "15 to 15 Roof."
(The roof position in a ladder company refers to one of the members who opens a hole in the roof so heat and smoke can escape a fire building)
Ladder 15 Roof: "15 Roof."
Ladder 15: "We got reports of another incoming plane. We may have to take cover. Stay in the stairwell."
Ladder 15 Roof: "10-4."
Ladder 15: "15 to 15 Roof. That plane's ours. I repeat: it's ours. What floor are you on, Scotty?"
Ladder 15 Roof: "54."
Ladder 15: "Alright. Keep making your way up. We're behind you."
Ladder 15 Roof: "10-4."

9:37 a.m.
Ladder 15 Lieutenant: "Tommy, listen carefully. I'm sending all the injured down to you on [floor] 40. You're going to have to get 'em down to the elevator. There's about 10 to 15 people coming down to you."
Ladder 15 OV: "Okay."
Ladder 15 Lieutenant: "Ten civilians coming down. Fifteen to OV."

Ladder 15 OV: "Got that, I'm on 40 right now, Lieu."
(OV refers to the firefighter assigned to the outside vent position – who would also help vent the building)

9:39 a.m.
Ladder 15 Lieutenant: "Alright Tommy, when you take people down to the lobby, try to get an EMS crew back."
Ladder 15 Firefighter: "Definitely."

9:43 a.m.
Battalion 7 Chief: "Battalion 7 to Ladder 15 Roof, what's your progress?"
Ladder 15 Roof: "[Floor] 63, Battalion."
Battalion 7 Chief: "10-4."
Battalion 9 Chief: "Battalion 9 to Battalion 7."
Battalion 7 Chief: "Go ahead Battalion 9."
Battalion 9 Chief: "Orio, I couldn't find a [elevator] bank to bring you up any higher. I'm on the 40th floor, what can I do for you?"
Battalion 7 Chief: "We're going to have to hoof it. I'm on 69 now, but we need a higher bank, K."
("K" refers to the end of a radio transmission)

Battalion 9 Chief: "What stairway you in, Orio?"
Battalion 7 Chief: "The center of the building, boy, boy…Battalion 7 to Ladder 15 Roof, what floor?"
Battalion 9 Chief: "Battalion 9 to Battalion 7."
Battalion 7 Chief: "…Battalion 9."
Battalion 9 Chief: "Orio, I'm going to try and get a couple of CFRD engines on the 40th floor so send any victims down here, I'll start up a staging area."
(CFRD refers to firefighters trained as Certified First Responders in Defibrillation)

Battalion 7 Chief: "…find a fireman service elevator close to 40, if we get some more cars in that bank, we'll be alright."

9:48 a.m.
Ladder 15: "15 to Battalion 7."
Battalion 7: "Go Ladder 15."
Ladder 15: "What do you got up there, Chief?"
Battalion 7 Chief: "I'm still in boy stair 74th floor. No smoke or fire problems, walls are breached, so be careful."

Ladder 15: "Yeah 10-4, I saw that on 68. Alright, we're on 71 we're coming up behind you."
Battalion 7 Chief: "10-4. Six more to go."
Ladder 15: "Let me know when you see more fire."
Battalion 7 Chief: "I found a [fire] marshal on 75."

9:49 a.m.

Ladder 15: "15 to 15 OV. 15 to 15 OV."
Ladder 15 OV: "15 OV."
Ladder 15: "Tommy, have you made it back down to the lobby yet?"
Ladder 15 OV: "The elevator's screwed up."
Ladder 15: "You can't move it?"
Ladder 15 OV: "I don't want to get stuck in the shaft."
(The firefighter who had waited on the 40th floor for the injured patients has loaded them into what had been the only working elevator, which is now stuck, to get them down to the lobby; officials had similarly hoped to bring firefighters up to the 40th floor so more personnel could help the injured)

9:50 a.m.

Ladder 15: "Alright Tommy. It's imperative that you go down to the lobby command post and get some people up to 40. We got injured people up here on 70. If you make it to the lobby command post, see if they can somehow get elevators past the 40th floor. We got people injured all the way up here."
Battalion 7 Aide: "Battalion 7 Alpha to 7."
Battalion 7 Chief: "Go Steve."
Battalion 7 Aide: "Yeah Chief, I'm on 55, I got to rest. I'll try to get up there as soon as possible."
Battalion 7 Chief: "10-4."

9:52 a.m.

Battalion 7 Chief: "Battalion 7 ... Ladder 15, we've got two isolated pockets of fire. We should be able to knock it down with two lines. Radio that, 78th floor numerous 10-45 code ones."
(10-45 is the Fire Department signal for an injured civilian. Various codes ranging from one to four indicate severity. A code one is someone who is deceased)

Ladder 15: "What stair are you in, Orio?"
Battalion 7 Aide: "7 Alpha to lobby command post."
Ladder 15: "15 to Battalion 7."
Battalion 7 Chief: "... Ladder 15."
Ladder 15: "Chief, what stair you in?"
Battalion 7 Chief: "South stairway Adam, South Tower."

Ladder 15: "Floor 78?"
Battalion 7 Chief: "10-4, numerous civilians, we gonna need two engines up here."
Ladder 15: "Alright 10-4, we're on our way."
…
Battalion 7 Aide: "7 Alpha for Battalion 7."
Battalion 7 Chief: "South tower, Steve, south tower, tell them…Tower one…Battalion 7 to Ladder 15."
Ladder 15: "15."
Battalion 7 Chief: "I'm going to need two of your firefighters [in] Adam Stairway.."
Ladder 15: "Alright 10-4, we're coming up the stairs. We're on 77 now in the B stair, I'll be right to you."
Ladder 15 Roof: "15 Roof to 15. We're on 71. We're coming right up."

9:57 a.m.

Battalion 9: "Alright, I'm on my way up Orio."
Ladder 15 OV: "15 OV to 15."
Ladder 15: "Go ahead 15 OV, Battalion 7 Operations Tower One."
Ladder 15 OV: "Stuck in the elevator, in the elevator shaft, you're going to have to get a different elevator. We're chopping through the wall to get out."
Battalion 7 Chief: "Radio lobby command with that Tower One."

9:58 a.m.

Battalion 7 Chief: "Battalion 7 to Ladder 15."

(end of tape)

9:59 a.m.

Tower Two collapses

"I pulled my helmet down and my coat up and I just thought I was going to die. I mean, everything started coming down and it turned black and there was just this noise of everything coming down…I just thought, 'I'm going to die.' I thought, 'This is it'…Then it seemed like, as each second or moment passed, I kept thinking, 'Well, I'm not dead yet, I'm not dead yet, I'm not dead yet' and then there was silence and it finally stopped falling, but it was pitch black and there was all this stuff in the air and I thought, 'Oh, now we're probably buried. This will be the final thing. You'll survive, but you'll be trapped.'"

— *Chief Medical Officer Kerry Kelly*

"It got very black. It got very quiet. It was very peacefully quiet, so peaceful that I thought I was dead…I didn't see anybody…Really it was like a ghost street. There was nobody there. I didn't see people."
— *Retired Assistant Commissioner Stephen Gregory*

"It is impossible to measure how many more civilians would have died but for the determination of many members of the FDNY, PAPD and NYPD to continue assisting civilians after the South Tower collapsed. It is impossible to measure the calming influence that ascending firefighters had on descending civilians or whether but for the firefighters' presence the poor behavior of a very few civilians could have caused a dangerous and panicked mob flight. But the positive impact of the first responders on the evacuation came at a tremendous cost of first responder lives lost."

— *The 9/11 Commission Report*

"We were there for a while trying to just catch people as they were coming out, people were being carried out, limping up. Everybody was pretty banged up, although not as banged up as I expected. I think a lot of us really expected worse injuries. It seemed like people were mostly either walking wounded or they didn't get out. It's unfortunate."
— *EMS Lieutenant Tracey Mulqueen*

FDNY 2001-2011: *A Decade of Remembrance and Resilience*

7 World Trade Center collapsed at 5:20 pm., more than seven hours after the collapse of both towers

FDNY 2001-2011: *A Decade of Remembrance and Resilience*

"For the first week or so, everybody – you couldn't pull people away if you tried. Everybody wanted to be there. They couldn't do enough, but it had come to a point where you had a decision to make that this is going to be a long-term operation. This stuff is not going to go away tomorrow."
— *EMS Chief Rosario Terranova*

The World Trade Center Ribbons Campaign

To recognize the extraordinary heroism and dedication exhibited by FDNY members of all ranks during, immediately thereafter and following the World Trade Center incident of September 11, 2001, the Fire Department initiated a one-time bestowal of ribbons to honor our members' actions. The three levels are:

Survivor: for those members who were on-scene and survived as the Towers collapsed.

Rescuer: for those members who operated within 24 hours after the Towers collapsed until the last rescue.

Campaign: for those members who participated in the rescue/recovery efforts.

"I've been cited five times for bravery, but the significance of September 11th and the memory of those lost, in my mind, made the World Trade Center Service Ribbon the most important one anyone could ever wear. It was the only one I wore."
– *Fire Commissioner Salvatore J. Cassano*

"As a kid I've always been amazed by those buildings…It's a part of our identity as New Yorkers. To see the skyline without those buildings, especially the first few weeks coming back to work with the smoke – that smoke didn't stop for a good month and a half after – it was totally unreal, totally unreal…I just feel sorry for everybody that was out there. I dedicate my career, the rest of my career in the Fire Department to the people that died that day."

— Firefighter Jody Bell

"Each day, making the turn onto West Street and walking toward the pile, I felt very small. I felt like it was an insignificant thing I was doing – 10,000 ants moving dirt…The size of the objects we were attempting to move were well beyond our capability. There were i-beams three feet high that went on for 40, 50 or 60 feet – they may as well have asked you to move a battleship…I've been to a thousand collapses and I've taken out members that were dead before, but this was of a scale that you knew you could not compensate for."

—*Retired Captain Philip Ruvolo*

"My wife and I lived a couple of blocks from the site and our apartment was filled with the smell of pulverized concrete and lost souls. I also worked there during the day, so it was like we never left the scene. We got used to the sounds of the machines there during the night and every time we heard them stop, we knew what that meant: They had found another body."

— *Firefighter Dan Potter*

"After the attacks, the Bureau of Fire Investigation's mission was expanded from fire investigation to helping recover Department property and personal effects. Most importantly, we were tasked with manning the Medical Examiner's office to help identify and recover the remains of our members, often using DNA. This meant going to private homes, dentists and doctors' offices for samples, which aided in identifying our fallen members. We established a temporary morgue in the old American Express building, in addition to the Medical Examiner's office, and Fire Marshals were assigned to both locations around the clock, until the recovery effort ended and the site closed."

– *Chief Fire Marshal Robert Byrnes*

"We spent most of the days looking for people. You're not talking about a body or even a torso, you're looking for even a finger…Anything that could represent a person, represent humanity…You could spend an hour, two hours or four hours to try to get that person out. And that was still a person, even though it was just a part of a person. And you had to treat that with total respect. That was the work for nine months."

—Retired Firefighter Lee Ielpi
The body of his son, Firefighter Jonathan Ielpi, was found three months after the September 11th attacks

"On January 1, 2002, my first day as Fire Commissioner, my wife Susan and I went from the inauguration to the World Trade Center site. There, amid the devastation of 9/11, we saw what loss and grief looks like up close. It was in the faces of the small group of fathers who were spending that New Years' Day the same way they had spent every day following the attacks: searching the wreckage and debris for the remains of their sons."
— *Former Fire Commissioner Nicholas Scoppetta*

FDNY 2001-2011: *A Decade of Remembrance and Resilience* | 47

"But yeah, my heart goes out to them. I thank God every day that I'm here. There's days I wonder why I'm here, why was I spared when others had so many – I'm not married, don't have any children, but others did. So there are days I wonder why me, why not somebody else. I guess it wasn't my time, but sometimes I ask why."
— *EMS Lieutenant Karen Lamanna*

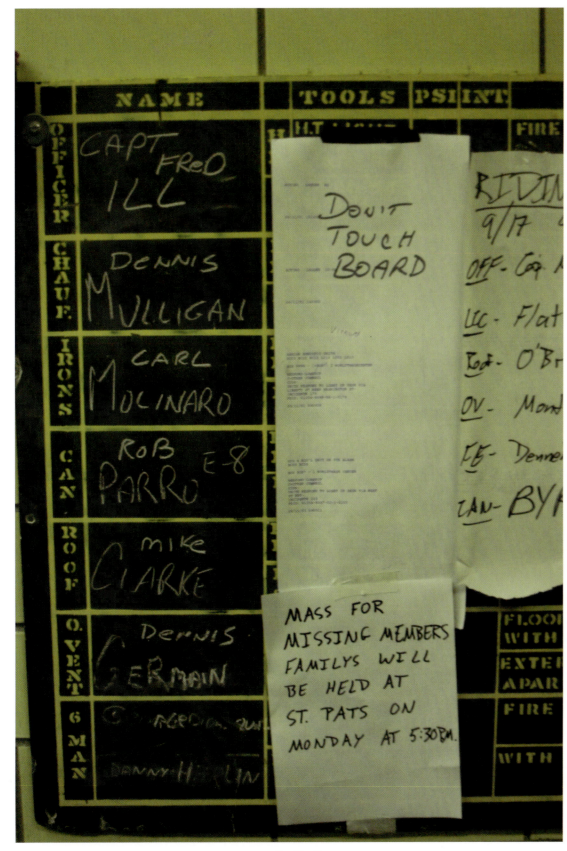

Ladder 2

"In every firehouse, there's a board listing all of the members scheduled to work that day. In some cases, September 11 wiped out entire companies. The boards became memorials to those we lost."

— *Fire Commissioner Salvatore J. Cassano*

FDNY 2001-2011: *A Decade of Remembrance and Resilience* | 49

"That first night it took two or three hours and 12 guys to get one piece of steel off one guy. But the next morning we came down West Street, and as far as we could see, it was all iron workers, steel workers, construction workers. These guys knew what to do, they knew how to move the steel. They were awesome. They did a great job. The whole country did a great job."

— *Retired Captain Mike Meagher*

"On one day in March we found 19 or 20 members. We got what was left and just carried them out."
— Lieutenant Kevin McCutchan

"All of the rescuers knew how important it was to operate safely around the fires and twisted metal. Despite incredibly difficult conditions, the Department can be proud that there were no serious injuries incurred during the months of digging and searching."
— *Chief of Department Edward S. Kilduff*

FDNY 2001-2011: *A Decade of Remembrance and Resilience* | 53

"Immediately after the attacks, FDNY and its Bureau of Health Services knew we had a responsibility to provide all of our members with the best medical care and monitoring as well as counseling. In the decade since, our doctors have provided medical monitoring exams to over 15,500 active and retired firefighters and EMS members. We have also treated over 10,000 for WTC-related physical and mental health issues and offered counseling to over 2,000 family members."

– *Dr. David Prezant,
Chief Medical Officer, FDNY*

- **98% of FDNY rescue workers lost someone they knew on September 11, 2001**
- **68% lost close friends at FDNY**
- **52% lost acquaintances at FDNY**
- **7% lost relatives at FDNY**

FDNY 2001-2011: *A Decade of Remembrance and Resilience*

2001-2011: *A Decade of Remembrance and Re*

"I remember going up and down West Street…[and] the people lined up supporting everybody. I think that was so important…for our own people. [Civilians] were showing up with flags, clapping; signs, 'We love you.' It was so supportive. That went on for the longest time, into the wee hours, every day, every night… It gave them the energy to go back down there and do something that nobody really ever thought they would have to do and dig out their own and try to find people alive. That helped [our] people…they knew whatever the end result was they were going to be appreciated."

— *EMS Chief Frances Pascale*

FDNY 2001-2011: *A Decade of Remembrance and Resilience*

60 | FDNY 2001-2011: *A Decade of Remembrance and Resilience*

FDNY 2001-2011: *A Decade of Remembrance and Resilience*

Funeral of Father Mychal Judge, September 15, 2001

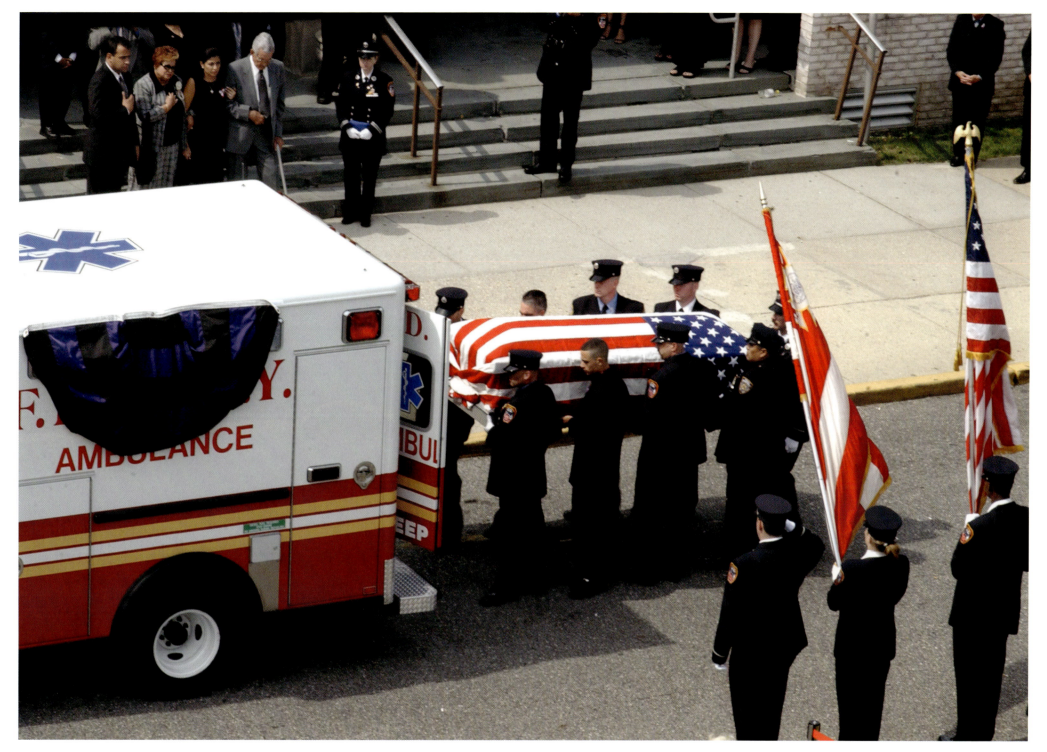

Funeral of Paramedic Carlos Lillo, September 14, 2002

"In June of 2001, three of our firefighters were killed on Fathers Day and we couldn't imagine a sadder thing. Who would have believed that less than three months later our losses would be compounded 100 times over...One Saturday shortly after September 11th, 27 funerals and memorial services were being conducted in a single day. Our Ceremonial Unit made certain FDNY was represented at each one."
— Lenore Koehler FDNY Events Director

Funeral of Lieutenant Kevin Dowdell, April 20, 2002

FDNY Memorial Day at Madison Square Garden, October 12, 2002

The Last Beam: Recovery Efforts End

May 28, 2002

"The last steel beam removed from the site marked a major milestone. For us, the strength of that beam would always signify the strength of our City and our Department."
— *Fire Commissioner Salvatore J. Cassano*

FDNY 2001-2011: *A Decade of Remembrance and Resilience* | 67

WTC site closes, May 30, 2002

68 | **FDNY 2001-2011:** *A Decade of Remembrance and Resilience*

FDNY 2001-2011: *A Decade of Remembrance and Resilience*

Fire Academy

Rescue 5/Engine 160

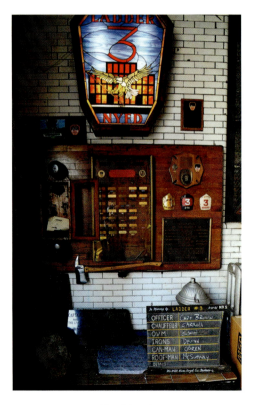

Ladder 3

Rescue 3

Engine 24/Ladder 5/Battalion 2

Engine 201/Ladder 114

Rescue 4/Engine 292

Engine 4/Ladder 15

Engine 157/Ladder 80

Engine 55

Engine 226

FDNY 2001-2011: *A Decade of Remembrance and Resilience*

Engine 8/Ladder 2/Battalion 8

Engine 26

Engine 23

72 | FDNY 2001-2011: *A Decade of Remembrance and Resilience*

Fort Totten

Fire Academy

Faces of the Fallen:
Members Lost on September 11, 2001

*FF Joseph Agnello, L-118	Lt. Brian G. Ahearn, E-230	FF Eric T. Allen, SQ-18	FF Richard D. Allen, L-15	*Capt. James M. Amato, SQ-1	FF Calixto Anaya, Jr., E-4	FF Joseph J. Angelini, Sr., R-1	FF Joseph J. Angelini, Jr., L-4	FF Faustino Apostol, Jr., Bn-2	FF David G. Arce, E-33	FF Louis Arena, L-5	FF Carl F. Asaro, Bn-9	Lt. Gregg Atlas, E-10
FF Gerald T. Atwood, L-21	FF Gerard Baptiste, L-9	AC Gerard A. Barbara, CWTC	FF Matthew E. Barnes, L-25	FF Arthur T. Barry, L-15	Lt. Steven J. Bates, E-235	*FF Carl J. Bedigian, E-214	FF Stephen E. Belson, L-24	FF John P. Bergin, R-5	FF Paul M. Beyer, E-6	FF Peter A. Bielfeld, L-42	FF Brian E. Bilcher, E-33	FF Carl V. Bini, R-5
FF Christopher J. Blackwell, R-3	FF Michael L. Bocchino, Bn-48	FF Frank J. Bonomo, E-230	FF Gary R. Box, SQ-1	FF Michael Boyle, E-33	FF Kevin H. Bracken, E-40	FF Michael E. Brennan, L-4	FF Peter Brennan, SQ-288	Capt. Daniel J. Brethel, L-24	Capt. Patrick J. Brown, L-3	FF Andrew C. Brunn, L-5	Capt. Vincent E. Brunton, L-105	FM Ronald P. Bucca, Man. Base
FF Greg J. Buck, E-201	Capt. William F. Burke, Jr., E-21	AC Donald J. Burns, CWTC	FF John P. Burnside, L-20	FF Thomas M. Butler, SQ-1	FF Patrick D. Byrne, L-101	FF George C. Cain, L-7	FF Salvatore B. Calabro, L-101	Capt. Frank J. Callahan, L-35	FF Michael F. Cammarata, L-11	FF Brian Cannizzaro, L-101	FF Dennis M. Carey, Haz-Mat 1	FF Michael S. Carlo, E-230
FF Michael T. Carroll, L-3	FF Peter J. Carroll, SQ-1	FF Thomas A. Casoria, E-22	FF Michael J. Cawley, L-136	FF Vernon P. Cherry, L-118	FF Nicholas P. Chiofalo, E-235	FF John G. Chipura, E-219	FF Michael J. Clarke, L-2	FF Steven Coakley, E-217	FF Tarel Coleman, SQ-252	FF John M. Collins, L-25	FF Robert J. Cordice, SQ-1	FF Ruben D. Correa, E-74
FF James R. Coyle, L-3	FF Robert J. Crawford, SFTY Bn-1	Lt. John A. Crisci, Haz-Mat 1	BC Dennis A. Cross, Bn-57	FF Thomas P. Cullen, III, SQ-41	FF Robert Curatolo, L-16	Lt. Edward A. D'Atri, SQ-1	FF Michael D. D'Auria, E-40	FF Scott M. Davidson, L-118	FF Edward J. Day, L-11	BC Thomas P. DeAngelis (1), Bn-8	*FF Manuel Del Valle, E-5	FF Martin N. DeMeo, Haz-Mat 1

74   FDNY 2001-2011: *A Decade of Remembrance and Resilience*

FF David P. DeRubbio, E-226	Lt. Andrew J. Desperito, E-1	BC Dennis L. Devlin, D-3	FF Gerard P. Dewan, L-3	FF George DiPasquale, L-2	Lt. Kevin W. Donnelly, L-3	Lt. Kevin C. Dowdell, R-4	*BC Raymond M. Downey, SOC	FF Gerard J. Duffy, L-21	Capt. Martin J. Egan, Jr., L-118	FF Michael J. Elferis, E-22	FF Francis Esposito, E-235	*Lt. Michael A. Esposito, SQ-1
FF Robert E. Evans, E-33	BC John J. Fanning (2), Haz-Mat Ops.	*Capt. Thomas J. Farino, E-26	FF Terrence P. Farrell, R-4	*Capt. Joseph D. Farrelly, E-4	First Deputy Comm. William M. Feehan	FF Lee S. Fehling, E-235	FF Alan D. Feinberg, Bn-9	FF Michael C. Fiore, R-5	*Lt. John R. Fischer, L-20	†FF Andre G. Fletcher, R-5	FF John J. Florio, E-214	Lt. Michael N. Fodor, L-21
FF Thomas J. Foley, R-3	*FF David J. Fontana, SQ-1	FF Robert J. Foti, L-7	*FF Andrew A. Fredericks, SQ-18	Lt. Peter L. Freund, E-55	FF Thomas Gambino, Jr., R-3	Chief of Dept. Peter J. Ganci, Jr.	Lt. Charles W. Garbarini, L-61	FF Thomas A. Gardner, Haz-Mat 1	FF Matthew D. Garvey, SQ-1	FF Bruce H. Gary, E-40	FF Gary P. Geidel, R-1	*BC Edward F. Geraghty, Bn-9
FF Denis P. Germain, L-2	*Lt. Vincent F. Giammona, L-5	FF James A. Giberson, L-35	*FF Ronnie E. Gies, SQ-288	FF Paul J. Gill, E-54	Lt. John F. Ginley, E-40	FF Jeffrey J. Giordano, L-3	FF John J. Giordano (1), E-37	FF Keith A. Glascoe, L-21	FF James M. Gray, L-20	BC Joseph Grzelak, Bn-48	FF Jose A. Guadalupe, E-54	Lt. Geoffrey E. Guja, E-82
Lt. Joseph P. Gullickson, L-101	*FF David Halderman, SQ-18	Lt. Vincent G. Halloran, L-8	FF Robert W. Hamilton, SQ-41	FF Sean S. Hanley, L-20	FF Thomas P. Hannafin, L-5	FF Dana R. Hannon, E-26	FF Daniel E. Harlin, L-2	Lt. Harvey L. Harrell, R-5	Lt. Stephen G. Harrell, L-10	*Capt. Thomas T. Haskell, Jr., L-132	FF Timothy S. Haskell, SQ-18	Capt. Terence S. Hatton, R-1
FF Michael H. Haub, L-4	Lt. Michael K. Healey, SQ-41	FF John F. Heffernan, L-11	FF Ronnie L. Henderson, E-279	FF Joseph P. Henry, L-21	FF William L. Henry, R-1	FF Thomas J. Hetzel, L-13	*Capt. Brian C. Hickey, R-4	Lt. Timothy B. Higgins, SQ-252	FF Jonathan R. Hohmann, Haz-Mat 1	FF Thomas P. Holohan, E-6	FF Joseph G. Hunter, SQ-288	Capt. Walter G. Hynes, L-13
FF Jonathan L. Ielpi, SQ-288	Capt. Frederick J. Ill, Jr., L-2	FF William R. Johnston, E-6	FF Andrew B. Jordan, L-132	FF Karl H. Joseph, E-207	Lt. Anthony M. Jovic, L-34	FF Angel L. Juarbe, Jr., L-12	Chaplain Mychal Judge	†FF Vincent D. Kane, E-22	*BC Charles L. Kasper, SOC	FF Paul H. Keating, L-5	FF Richard J. Kelly, Jr., L-11	*FF Thomas R. Kelly, L-105

FDNY 2001-2011: A Decade of Remembrance and Resilience

Lt. Glenn C. Perry, L-25 | Lt. Philip S. Petti, L-12 | Lt. Kevin J. Pfeifer, E-33 | Lt. Kenneth J. Phelan, E-217 | FF Christopher J. Pickford, E-201 | FF Shawn E. Powell, E-207 | FF Vincent A. Princiotta, L-7 | FF Kevin M. Prior, SQ-252 | BC Richard A. Prunty, Bn-2 | FF Lincoln Quappe, R-2 | Lt. Michael T. Quilty, L-11 | Paramedic Ricardo J. Quinn, EMS Bn-57 | FF Leonard J. Ragaglia, E-54

FF Michael P. Ragusa, E-279 | FF Edward J. Rall, R-2 | FF Adam D. Rand, SQ-288 | FF Donald J. Regan, R-3 | Lt. Robert M. Regan, L-118 | FF Christian Regenhard, L-131 | FF Kevin O. Reilly, E-207 | *Lt. Vernon A. Richard, L-7 | FF James C. Riches, E-4 | FF Joseph R. Rivelli, Jr., L-25 | FF Michael E. Roberts, E-214 | FF Michael E. Roberts, L-35 | FF Anthony Rodriguez, E-279

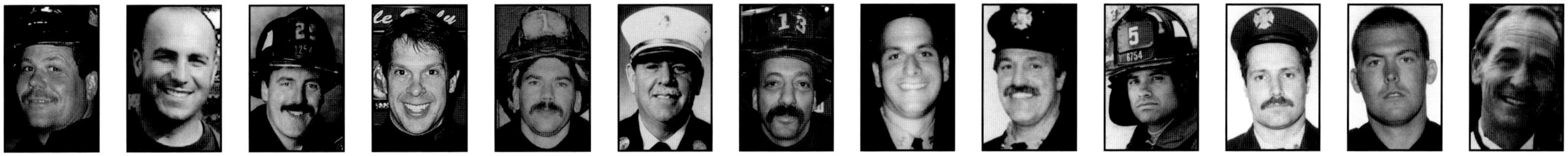

FF Matthew S. Rogan, L-11 | FF Nicholas P. Rossomando, R-5 | FF Paul G. Ruback, L-25 | FF Stephen Russell, E-55 | Lt. Michael T. Russo, SQ-1 | BC Matthew L. Ryan, Bn-4 | FF Thomas E. Sabella, L-13 | FF Christopher A. Santora, E-54 | FF John A. Santore, L-5 | FF Gregory T. Saucedo, L-5 | FF Dennis Scauso, Haz-Mat 1 | FF John A. Schardt, E-201 | BC Fred C. Scheffold, Bn-12

FF Thomas G. Schoales, E-4 | FF Gerard P. Schrang, R-3 | FF Gregory R. Sikorsky, SQ-41 | FF Stephen G. Siller, SQ-1 | FF Stanley S. Smagala, Jr., E-226 | FF Kevin J. Smith, Haz-Mat 1 | FF Leon Smith, Jr., L-118 | FF Robert W. Spear, Jr., E-26 | FF Joseph P. Spor, R-3 | BC Lawrence T. Stack, SFTY Bn-1 | Capt. Timothy M. Stackpole, L-103 | FF Gregory M. Stajk, L-13 | FF Jeffrey Stark, E-230

FF Benjamin Suarez, L-21 | FF Daniel T. Suhr, E-216 | Lt. Christopher P. Sullivan, L-111 | FF Brian E. Sweeney, R-1 | FF Sean P. Tallon, L-10 | FF Allan Tarasiewicz, R-5 | FF Paul A. Tegtmeier, E-4 | FF John P. Tierney, L-9 | FF John J. Tipping, II, L-4 | FF Hector L. Tirado, Jr., E-23 | FF Richard B. Van Hine, SQ-41 | FF Peter A. Vega, L-118 | FF Lawrence G. Veling, E-235

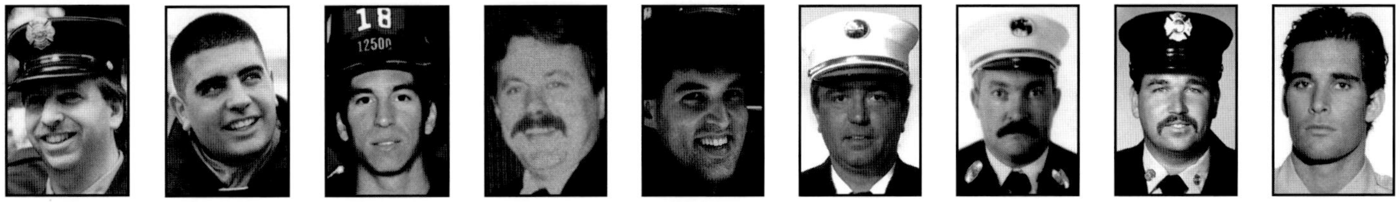

FF John T. Vigiano, II, L-132 | FF Sergio G. Villanueva, L-132 | FF Lawrence J. Virgilio, SQ-18 | Lt. Robert F. Wallace, E-205 | *FF Jeffrey P. Walz, L-9 | Lt. Michael P. Warchola, L-5 | Capt. Patrick J. Waters (2), Haz-Mat 1 | FF Kenneth T. Watson, E-214 | FF Michael T. Weinberg, E-1

FF David M. Weiss, R-1 | FF Timothy M. Welty, SQ-288 | FF Eugene M. Whelan, E-230 | FF Edward J. White, E-230 | FF Mark P. Whitford, E-23 | Lt. Glenn E. Wilkinson, E-238 | BC John P. Williamson, Bn-6 | Capt. David T. Wooley, L-4 | FF Raymond R. York, E-285

* Promoted to the next rank, effective September 10, 2001.

† Promoted to Fire Marshal, effective September 10, 2001.

FDNY 2001-2011: *A Decade of Remembrance and Resilience* 77

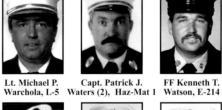

FDNY 2001-2011: A Decade of Remembrance and Resilience

by Fire Commissioner Salvatore J. Cassano

On September 11th 2001, I had been a firefighter for over thirty years. I had fought a lot fires and worked through the busiest and toughest years the Department had ever faced. I thought I had seen it all. I was wrong.

The day before the towers came down, the beloved FDNY Chaplain Father Mychal Judge reminded us that in this job, we never really know what to expect. That morning, he was in the Bronx at Engine 73 and Ladder 42, rededicating the renovated firehouse. There, he gave an inspiring sermon that was also strangely foreshadowing: "You have no idea, when you get on that rig, what God is calling you to do."

Not even 24 hours after he spoke those words, the World Trade Center was attacked, and Father Judge was one of the first killed. The Department was changed, the City was changed, the whole world was changed. And most significantly for us, September 11th changed the lives of the 343 FDNY families who lost loved ones.

In this Department, nobody was left untouched by the violence. I lost my closest friend. I lost my mentor. And, for a short time, I lost faith. I lost faith that we would ever be able to recover from such a devastating blow.

Then, a few weeks after the attacks, my faith was restored. I had just returned home from the site, where our members were carrying out the heartbreaking work of recovering victims. It was the middle of the night when I was sitting at my kitchen table and a call came over my department radio. The Manhattan dispatcher transmitted box 815, for a run in Midtown. Within seconds, Engine 54 – a company that had lost their entire crew at the World Trade Center – came on the radio and replied: "Engine 54 to Manhattan. We are available for that box." I heard that and I knew that we were going to be okay. Despite the terrible losses Engine 54/Ladder 4 had suffered, they were still ready, willing and able to go to work. We were bloodied – but we were not broken.

After the attack on our nation, as we in the Department focused on rebuilding, the men and women of the United States Armed Forces went to work in our names, to root out and destroy the terrorist networks that had caused so much suffering. Their mission to bring us justice came to fruition with the death of Osama bin Laden on May 1, 2011. But their noble work came at a huge cost, and the sacrifices that our military personnel and their families have borne in the last ten years must be recognized. Few appreciate it more than members of the FDNY. We thank our military personnel and we also thank President Bush and President Obama for staying the course and making sure justice was done for our families.

Almost ten years after the attacks, Engine 54/Ladder 4 – the same company that restored my faith nine years earlier – would play a pivotal role in another terrorist attack, when a car bomb was left in Times Square. As soon as they arrived on scene, they realized this was not a routine call. Before Sept. 11th, our members may have rushed to put out the fire without considering other factors. But thanks to the many changes we have made since the attacks on the World Trade Center, Engine 54/Ladder 4 were armed with good instincts, good training and good technology. Their decision not to put water on the fire preserved evidence that led to the would-be terrorist's capture. They called the bomb squad and helped clear the area. They knew exactly what to do, as well as what not to do.

September 11th was a paradigm shift for us. Firefighting had always been a very dangerous job: in the nine months before the World Trade Center attacks, seven members were killed in the line of duty. But before Sept. 11th, our firefighters were trained to respond, for the most part, to unintentional acts. Suddenly, we faced the reality of responding to an attack deliberately designed to kill thousands of people, including first responders.

To prepare for the new reality, we enhanced our members' skills by increasing training at every level. We expanded training for all firefighters with extra focus on HazMat, disaster preparedness, building construction and inspections. We implemented high-level management training for our officers and sent others to a ten-week West Point Counter-Terrorism course.

We built a state-of-the-art Operations Center that allows us to better manage large-scale disasters using real time data from state, local, national and international sources. We obtained new protective masks as well as radiation detectors and protective suits for hazardous materials.

We're also doing more than ever to keep our members safe and prepared for dangers in the field. We developed personal safety system ropes, allowing firefighters trapped in a burning building to safely descend from a window, and we greatly improved fire ground accountability systems so that we can safely track our members at the scene of an incident.

We also readied our infrastructure, installing Automatic Vehicle Locator technology to better dispatch ambulances, and improved our radio communications network.

We began our renowned World Trade Center Medical Monitoring and treatment program to care for all those who served at the disaster site. This information helped not only our members but the thousands of other workers, volunteers and residents who worked there.

The World Trade Center attacks left 607 Fire Department children without fathers; 16 babies were born to new widows during the recovery efforts. Spouses, parents, children and siblings formed a grieving community that numbered over 1300 people. To provide a center of support for the Sept. 11th families, the FDNY established the Family Assistance Unit to help with memorial services, paperwork, benefit information, college scholarships and more. Unfortunately, one unexpected consequence of the violence on Sept. 11th has been an increase in World Trade Center-related illness, and as of May 2011, 29 members have died from illnesses related to their service at the World Trade Center site. Ten years on, our Family Assistance unit continues to maintain close ties to all these Sept. 11th families, while also providing compassionate assistance to the families of currently active members when there is a loss or serious illness. And we greatly enhanced our Counseling Services Unit to help our members cope with emotional trauma.

As Father Judge said the day before the attacks, "Those of you who are working now, keep going."

And in the 10 years since the World Trade Center, that's exactly what we did. And now I am proud to say we are better prepared, better trained and better equipped than ever before.

It's what Father Judge would have wanted. It's what the 343 members who were lost on Sept. 11th would have wanted. As we continue to move forward, their sacrifice will never be forgotten – it is what gives us the strength and inspiration to carry on.

Members who died in the Line of Duty since September 11, 2001

EMT Andre Lahens
EMS Battalion 39
April 25, 2002

Firefighter James J. O'Shea
Ladder Company 127
September 27, 2003

Firefighter Thomas C. Brick
Ladder Company 36
December 16, 2003

Firefighter Christian P. Engeldrum†
Ladder Company 61
November 29, 2004

Lieutenant John J. Bellew
Ladder Company 27
January 23, 2005

Lieutenant Curtis W. Meyran
Battalion 26
January 23, 2005

Firefighter Richard T. Sclafani
Ladder Company 103
January 23, 2005

EMS Lieutenant Brendan D. Pearson
EMS Station 23
April 23, 2005

Firefighter Michael C. Reilly
Engine Company 75
August 27, 2006

Lieutenant Howard J. Carpluk Jr.
Engine Company 42
August 28, 2006

Firefighter Daniel F. Pujdak
Ladder Company 146
June 21, 2007

Lieutenant Joseph Graffagnino*
Ladder Company 5
August 18, 2007

Firefighter Robert Beddia
Engine Company 24
August 18, 2007

Lieutenant John H. Martinson
Engine Company 249
January 3, 2008

Firefighter Jamel M. Sears
Bureau of Training
Fire Academy
November 11, 2008

Lieutenant Robert J. Ryan, Jr.
Engine Company 155
November 23, 2008

Firefighter Paul Warhola
Engine Company 221
August 14, 2009

† Staff Sergeant US Army National Guard, 69th Infantry, Baghdad, Iraq

* Posthumously promoted

Rebuilding the Ranks

"Rebuilding the Department was our highest priority. The 91 destroyed engines, trucks and other equipment were quickly replaced. What could not be replaced was the 4,400 years of experience lost on 9/11. We tried to make up for that loss, and the surge in retirements, by stepping up hiring and training. The extraordinary men and women who joined the department after 9/11 lacked the experience of those who came before, but not the heart, courage and commitment."
-- *Former Fire Commissioner Nicholas Scoppetta*

Graduation of the first class of new firefighters to join FDNY after the attacks, December 31, 2001

The next class of probationary firefighters being sworn in to the Fire Academy on January 22, 2002

Crash of American Airlines Flight 587 in Rockaway, Queens – November 12, 2001

"It was one of my first days off after 9/11. I was walking my dog, Guinness, when I suddenly saw a plane overhead literally start to fall apart in the sky, spinning around out of control until it came crashing down into my neighborhood, about eight blocks away from where I was. I ran toward it and called my wife and told her, 'We've got another terrorist attack. A plane crashed.' A lot of firefighters live in that neighborhood so they and I were immediately on scene, evacuating homes in the surrounding areas and directing units as they arrived. It wasn't until much later that I realized it was just an accident."
— *Retired Chief of Department Peter Hayden*

Staten Island Ferry Crash – October 15, 2003

"On Oct. 15, 2003, the Staten Island ferry crashed, killing ten people and injuring many more. As I arrived at the site of the crash, EMTs from the FDNY had placed the dead and injured into ambulances and rushed off, sirens screaming. Firefighters were at work shoring up the damaged ferry slip. They worked with calm and efficiency, surrounded by what looked very much like a war zone."
— Fire Commissioner Salvatore J. Cassano

FDNY 2001-2011: *A Decade of Remembrance and Resilience* | 85

Fighting Fires

10-alarm, May 2, 2006, West Street, Brooklyn

5-alarm, August 6, 2008, East 180th Street, Bronx

3-alarm, January 26, 2009, 86-01 101st Avenue, Queens

3-alarm, December 5, 2004, 976 Decatur Street, Brooklyn

FDNY 2001-2011: *A Decade of Remembrance and Resilience*

4-alarm, September 24, 2002, 2916 3rd Avenue, Bronx

5-alarm, August 9, 2004, 1214 St. Nicholas Avenue, Manhattan

All-hands fire, April 12, 2004, 73rd Street, Brooklyn

3-alarm, January 23, 2004, 428 Avenue B, Manhattan

6-alarm, February 1, 2006, 1270 Gerard Avenue, Bronx

3-alarm, December 11, 2010, 118-47 Farmers Boulevard, Queens

Drills: Preparing for the Worst

"When we come to New York and work with the FDNY, we know we're training with pros. They're the best in the business."

— U.S. Marine Colonel John Pollock, Commanding Officer of the U.S. Marines' Chemical Biological Incident Response Force, at a drill with FDNY on April 22, 2010

April 22, 2010, Joint Drill with US Marines

October 17, 2010 Drill in Queens

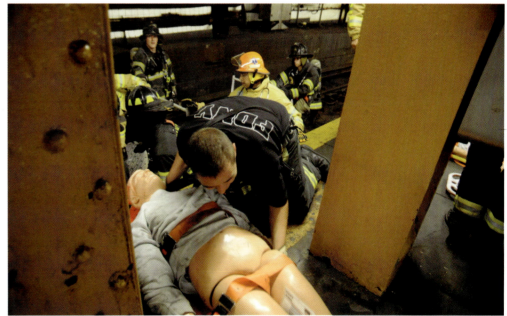

June 30, 2009 Subway Drill in Brooklyn

FDNY 2001–2011: *A Decade of Remembrance and Resilience*

East Side Crane Collapse – March 15, 2009

"It started off a beautiful day in early spring. People were in Central Park or sitting at outdoor cafes. We were heading back from a call when the dispatcher put out reports of a falling crane in midtown Manhattan. We arrived with the first-due units to a one-block scene of utter destruction – the pancake collapse of a 5-story building and a 9-story building with its entire side sheered off and the crane lying across the top. We went to work and were actually instrumental in the rescue of a civilian who survived. It took us two-and-a-half hours to tunnel through about 20-30 feet of concrete and steel to reach him."

—Lieutenant Tom Donnelly

"Someone who's been trapped under rubble for that long can't just be taken out. Being under that much weight changes the blood chemistry and, without the right medication, that can poison the rest of the body once you're released. My partner and I crawled through rubble to administer what's called 'crush medicine' that ultimately played a big role in two patients' survival."

— Rescue Paramedic Marco Girao

FDNY on the Water

"In 2010, we dedicated two 140-foot, $27 million fireboats to our marine fleet. Capable of pumping 50,000 gallons of water per minute and able to detect chemical, biological, radiological and nuclear agents, they play a crucial role protecting our busy harbor from terrorist threats. Both boats – Three Forty Three, named for the members lost on September 11th, and Fire Fighter II – stand as a powerful message to the world that the FDNY – indeed the whole city – is stronger than ever."

– Fire Commissioner Salvatore J. Cassano

FDNY 2001-2011: *A Decade of Remembrance and Resilience*

Giving Back: FDNY Responds to Hurricane Katrina

"After 9/11, first responders from all over the country came to New York to help. I felt like they kind of picked us up, dusted us off and got us back on our feet. At funerals and memorial services after 9/11, I saw members of the New Orleans Fire Department who had made the trip up to pay their respects and help any way they could. So when there was a call to go down to New Orleans and help after Hurricane Katrina hit in 2005, I jumped at the chance."

— *Captain Liam Flaherty*

98 | FDNY 2001-2011: *A Decade of Remembrance and Resilience*

Helping Haiti

"My father, who was killed on September 11th, helped create the program that brought our team to Haiti after the 2010 earthquake. That made our work even more rewarding for me. But it was also incredibly challenging – mass devastation, untold numbers of dead and no infrastructure – making this the worst environment we've ever operated in. But we worked hard and we saved several lives. The night we rescued two children, who had been trapped beneath three stories of rubble for seven days, meant so much to everybody."

— *Rescue Battalion Chief Joseph Downey,
son of Deputy Chief Raymond Downey*

FDNY 2001-2011: *A Decade of Remembrance and Resilience* | 101

Miracle on the Hudson

"After we rescued about 20 passengers off the wing and ferried them safely to shore, I told them, 'Welcome to New York.' One of the passengers said, 'We just left New York!'"
— *Retired Firefighter Thomas Sullivan on the January 15, 2009 Hudson River landing of US Airways flight 1549*

FDNY 2001-2011: *A Decade of Remembrance and Resilience* | 103

September 11th Families Making a Difference

"On September 11th, my brother, Firefighter Stephen Siller, had just gotten off work when he heard about the attacks. He returned to Squad 1 to get his gear and, when he was unable to drive through the Brooklyn Battery Tunnel, he got out and ran through with sixty pounds of gear on his back. We lost him that day, but each year thousands honor Stephen and the other 342 FDNY members lost on 9/11 at the Tunnel to Towers Run."

— *Russell Siller*

"Our brother was among the 343 lost in 2001. As a tribute to his memory, we created the Michael Lynch Foundation. Since 2002, we've granted over $1.6 million in scholarships to 75 young people. We know Michael would be very proud of that."
—Kathleen Lynch

"If 9/11 never happened, there's a good chance Walter Reed Army Medical Center would not be as busy as it is. The war started on September 11th. Our sons and the others lost that day were the first victims of that war. Young people are still joining the military because of that, so it's our obligation as parents and Americans to thank them and let them know we're supporting them."
— *Retired Captain John Vigiano, who lost both his sons, Firefighter John Vigiano Jr. and Police Officer Joseph Vigiano, on September 11th, explaining the 16 trips he has made to Water Reed*

Carrying on a Proud Legacy

These five firefighters all work together in Engine 255/Ladder 157 in Brooklyn. All of them lost close family members at the World Trade Center on September 11th. Firefighter Brendan Ielpi, brother of Firefighter Jonathan Ielpi; Firefighter Christopher Howard, son of Port Authority Officer George Howard; Firefighter Timothy Brunton, nephew of Captain Vincent Brunton; Firefighter Christopher Ganci, son of Chief of Department Peter Ganci; and Firefighter Andrew Esposito, son of Captain Michael Esposito.

Moments of Remembrance 2002-2010

September 11, 2010

September 11, 2002

September 11, 2003

September 11, 2008

FDNY 2001-2011: *A Decade of Remembrance and Resilience*

September 11, 2008, Fireman's Monument, Riverside Park

President Barack Obama places a wreath at the foot of the Survivor Tree on Memorial Plaza at the site of the September 11th Memorial and Museum at Ground Zero in New York, N.Y., May 5, 2011

FDNY 2001-2011: *A Decade of Remembrance and Resilience*

To support FDNY public safety efforts, please visit *www.fdnyfoundation.org*

The Fire Department would like to thank the photographers and news agencies who donated their photographs to help us tell our story.

The New York Times
Bill Cunningham
Chang W. Lee
Reuters
Shannon Stapleton
The Associated Press
Matt Moyer
The New York Daily News
David Handschuh
Todd Maisel
The White House
Chuck Kennedy

Chris Casciano
John Labriola
Todd Rengel
Steve Spak
Heather E. Smith

We would also like to thank Ralph Bernard, Randy Barron, David Warren, Kristin Eng, David Sherzer, Victoria Dunham, Frank Dwyer, FF John Leavy, Lt. Richard Smiouskas, FF Ben Cotton, FF Christopher Landano, and EMT Robert Domingo for helping with this project.